DSC SPEED READS

PERSONAL DEVELOPMENT

Managing Your Manager

Cathy Shimmin

directory of social change

Published by the Directory of Social Change (Registered Charity no. 800517 in England and Wales)

Registered address: Directory of Social Change, First Floor, 10 Queen Street Place, London EC4R 1BE

Tel: 020 4526 5995

Visit www.dsc.org.uk to find out more about our books, subscription funding website and training events. You can also sign up for e-newsletters so that you're always the first to hear about what's new.

The publisher welcomes suggestions and comments that will help to inform and improve future versions of this and all of our titles. Please give us your feedback by emailing publications@dsc.org.uk.

It should be understood that this publication is intended for guidance only and is not a substitute for professional advice. No responsibility for loss occasioned as a result of any person acting or refraining from acting can be accepted by the author or publisher.

Print and digital editions first published 2024

Copyright © Directory of Social Change 2024

All rights reserved. No part of the printed version of this book may be stored in a retrieval system or reproduced in any form whatsoever without prior permission in writing from the publisher. This book is sold subject to the condition that it shall not, by way of trade or otherwise, be lent, re-sold, hired out or otherwise circulated without the publisher's prior permission in any form of binding or cover other than that in which it is published, and without a similar condition including this condition being imposed on the subsequent purchaser.

The digital version of this publication may only be stored in a retrieval system for personal use. No part may be edited, amended, extracted or reproduced in any form whatsoever. It may not be distributed or made available to others without prior permission in writing from the publisher.

The publisher and author have made every effort to contact copyright holders. If anyone believes that their copyright material has not been correctly acknowledged, please contact the publisher, who will be pleased to rectify the omission.

The moral right of the author has been asserted in accordance with the Copyrights, Designs and Patents Act 1988.

ISBN 978 1 78482 096 1 (print edition)
ISBN 978 1 78482 097 8 (digital edition)

British Library Cataloguing in Publication Data
A catalogue record for this book is available from the British Library

Cover and text design by Kate Griffith
Printed and bound in the UK by Martins the Printers, Berwick upon Tweed

Contents

Introduction		4
Chapter 1:	Relationships matter	5
	▪ Bumps and battles	6
	▪ Drains and radiators	6
	▪ Where is the power?	8
Chapter 2:	What your manager needs	10
	▪ Understand your role	11
	▪ Communicate effectively	12
	▪ Show initiative	16
Chapter 3:	What you need	17
	▪ Your performance	18
	▪ Decision-making authority	20
	▪ Behaviour and conduct	21
Chapter 4:	Structured conversations	24
	▪ Conversation frameworks	25
	▪ Effective questions	26
Chapter 5:	Building resilience	29
	▪ Bullying and harassment	29
	▪ Managing stress	30
	▪ Resilience	31
	▪ Final note	32

Introduction

Who will this book help?

This book is for anyone who is managed and under the leadership of others, especially those new to the workplace. If you are a manager, this book may also be useful to help you empathise with, and get the best from, the people you manage.

What will it give you?

The relationship between you and your manager can sometimes become difficult – for many reasons. This book will help you work through the issues and offer some possible approaches to get this relationship back on track. Having a productive and professional relationship with your manager means you can contribute to, and influence, higher-level decision-making and policies that affect your working life. It also gives you the chance to learn from their knowledge and experience and develop in your role.

The book focuses on the line-management relationship but does so from the less obvious view of looking at managing *up* the line. It explores some of the inherent challenges in this relationship, for example making requests, getting recognition, giving and receiving feedback, agreeing priorities and working parameters, and managing expectations and boundaries. This book's goal is not to change who you or your manager are. It is *not* about 'winning' in this relationship but about having a winning relationship to achieve work goals.

Chapter 1

Relationships matter

This chapter looks at the dynamics of line-management relationships.

> **Case study – my story**
>
> At 20 years old, I worked in a clothes shop for a really useless manager. They moved the goalposts, deadlines and priorities on a whim. They said things like 'I need you to...' or 'You're my staff, so...' And they made snide remarks about other staff in their absence.
>
> I'd like to tell you it ended well and I completely turned them around to be a trusting, empowering, supportive manager and that's why I'm writing this book. But that didn't happen. I fought back, played games, and manipulated words and situations hoping to gain some power. I was sulky and sarcastic. I either worked to the bare minimum or went hell for leather to prove my worth. My behaviour only caused my manager to control me even more.
>
> The problem with my approach was that the behaviours I was demonstrating rarely help to fix things *and* they destroy our own credibility or character. Taking things personally and making things personal did nothing to help the relationship. And managing the relationship was precisely where the problem lay. I've since learned to focus on making relationships work and enjoyed a long career in the charity sector.

Bumps and battles

Most of the time, relationships at work are healthy, productive, even – dare I say it – fun. However, even in the best of relationships there are bumps: behaviours or incidents that make things difficult, fraught or frustrating. If you manage these things assertively and professionally, you will have a less stressful time at work and look more credible. It also means that bumps are less likely to become battles.

Any conflict in a relationship at work is a bumpy road to navigate, but when it is with your line manager, that presents a whole new road-user etiquette. How do you say no to your manager? How do you tell them that what they are doing, have done or are planning to do has flaws without straining the relationship? How do you say 'I don't understand' or 'I don't agree' without being seen as untrustworthy or losing credibility in others' eyes? How do you get recognition or rewards without looking needy, or get constructive feedback rather than getting a negative verbal battering?

> **Where next?**
> For more on working with others, see *The Pleasure and the Pain*, Debra Allcock Tyler, DSC, 2007.

Drains and radiators

The key point in the case study at the start of the chapter is that to minimise bumps and battles in any relationship, we can choose to drain energy or radiate possibility *within* that relationship. A helpful mantra at work is: 'If the relationship is good, all other things become possible.' We can't change other people, so it's not usually about you or them – it's all about the relationship you create between each other.

In positive relationships, there is positive energy, hope, trust and respect. These qualities don't exist by accident – one or both parties in the relationship need to work on creating them. So, do you radiate all these factors in your working relationships or do you drain them? Below is an exercise about the attitudes and beliefs you bring to your relationships.

Attitudes that foster effective relationships

The following attitudes foster effective relationships. Which feel reasonable to you, and which feel like a big ask?

Evaluate each statement on a scale of 1 (completely disagree) to 10 (completely agree).

Acceptance:
No one is perfect. Relationships need work.
 1 2 3 4 5 6 7 8 9 10

Ambition:
Possibilities are limitless. There is always a solution.
 1 2 3 4 5 6 7 8 9 10

Trust:
I am my word. I deliver on my word, and I will trust you to hold yours.
 1 2 3 4 5 6 7 8 9 10

Resolution:
Putting personal feelings aside, I commit to action/solution.
 1 2 3 4 5 6 7 8 9 10

Serenity:
Sometimes things will work out and sometimes they won't.
 1 2 3 4 5 6 7 8 9 10

Resilience:
When things don't work out, I can try something new.
 1 2 3 4 5 6 7 8 9 10

Higher scores indicate personal strengths in making relationships work, whereas lower scores suggest personal barriers. Consider what you can do to increase your strengths. For example, if you score 6 on 'Trust' – you believe you keep to your word but don't necessarily hold others to theirs – think about agreements, parameters or deadlines that will help you to ensure people keep their word. Seek training on how to be more assertive to help you approach someone who doesn't fulfil their promises.

Where is the power?

There is 'position power' within the hierarchies of most organisations. That is, someone has (or others perceive them to have) more power because they are in a more senior position than you are.

The person in the position of power (your manager) may not be easy to influence. You may need to navigate the situation carefully because of the established remits of responsibility and accountability. You don't always have the authority to take decisions, establish a course of action, change plans and so on without permission from those you are accountable to. For many aspects of an organisation's life, this makes sense and helps keep things robust and managed effectively.

> **Top tip**
> When a relationship is good, all other things become possible. Work on relationships and behaviours, not people and personalities.

However, whether or not you have position power, it is still possible to use effective leadership and influencing behaviours. This is your 'personal power'. This type of power allows you to reframe your attitude to difficult relationships, choose and use language and behaviour that is non-confrontational, and define and communicate your personal boundaries and expectations.

Here are three starting points for how you can use your personal power to create positive relationships:

- **Embrace and develop attitudes that support effective relationships.** Refer back to the exercise on page 7 to establish which attitudes you're already comfortable with and which will need work. Adjusting any negative attitudes towards the relationship opens up possibilities.
- **De-personalise things.** Centre conversations with your manager around the organisation's priorities and encourage your manager to do

the same. This way, any demands feel less like personal attacks or work being dumped on you. (The case study below illustrates this point from the manager's point of view.)

- **Define what a good relationship would look like for you.** Imagine your relationship a year from now. Things are going well. What are the characteristics of the relationship, how did it get to this point and what was within your control to influence the change?

> ### Case study – de-personalising things
>
> Mo was managing a project to improve a biannual publication by a charity. This included increasing the quality while decreasing the budget. To achieve this, Mo gave the team higher targets for selling advertising space in the publication (the charity used this to offset production costs). Before setting these targets, Mo researched what other organisations had achieved and checked similar publications (this showed that others included more advertising than their charity). Mo ensured their plan was not too rapid a departure from previous targets and consulted a senior colleague. They also offered extra sales support, and senior colleagues contributed leads.
>
> One member of Mo's team put up a lot of resistance and became rather difficult to work with. Mo asked to meet them to have an open conversation about what was going on. It transpired the colleague was upset Mo had been recently promoted to a role the other person felt *they* deserved. The colleague also had not understood that the new targets were based on organisational and not personal needs. The team member thought Mo was throwing their power around. Once Mo explained the new budget constraints and showed them their working, the other person was much happier (and exceeded their target). In fact, Mo and their former team member are still friends years later!

Chapter 2

What your manager needs

This chapter helps you to consider what your manager needs from you and how to provide it.

Your manager is accountable for you doing your work and is responsible for providing the resources with which you can do it. That accountability means that your manager needs certain things from you in order to be able to report to their manager up the line and to support you down the line.

You, in turn, are responsible for your work. That responsibility means that you need to deliver specified results. (It also means there are certain things you need from your manager too – chapter 3 covers that.)

Your manager needs:

- you to fulfil your job requirements and achieve set goals or targets;
- to understand what will help you achieve results;

> **Top tip**
> Ask yourself and your manager: 'What are the agreed targets, priorities and deadlines?'
> Clarity helps you to feel confident and to be able to negotiate around your own boundaries and expectations.

- to know what is getting in the way of you achieving results;
- a measure of your performance, for example fundraising income figures;
- your conduct to be in line with organisational values, standards of behaviour and policies.

Understand your role

A good starting point to meeting your manager's needs is to know your job and the scope of it. This doesn't just mean having the required competencies. After all, you may have ongoing learning, training or re-training needs. Clearly, your competency is required, but it's just as important to know the scope and dimensions of your job. What are you being measured on? What decision-making authority do you have? How do you decide priorities?

Your job description and your annual performance targets should outline your role requirements. If you don't have these, have a conversation with your manager to ensure you have a mutual understanding of what is expected of you. Chapter 4 gives some useful pointers to doing this assertively.

The main thing to remember is: you are both accountable to the people and purpose your organisation serves. This perspective avoids the 'working for my manager' thinking, which is not helpful in creating a balanced and equal relationship. It also means that when faced with a problem or a conflict situation, you can agree solutions that work best for the people you serve

> **Where next?**
>
> Acas's website offers some job description templates. Compare them with your role specifications to see what might be missing. Discuss with your manager your job description and if it needs updating. Mutual clarity will help everyone to travel in the same direction.
>
> *www.acas.org.uk/job-description-templates*

or that help your organisation achieve its purpose. This is really good common ground for both you and your manager to be starting from.

Communicate effectively

To understand what helps and hinders you achieving results, your manager needs to know what is going on, what has gone on and what might go on regarding the work you are responsible for. This might, from time to time, include personal life issues that could be getting in the way. It's up to you to decide what you feel is useful and appropriate to share.

> **Top tip**
> Use team meetings to talk about team-related matters and to contribute ideas to other projects and work.
> Use one-to-ones to talk about *your* work, *your* achievements and what concerns *you*.

Part of managing your manager means you need to regularly and clearly inform them of these things – don't wait to be asked. It's much easier for them to help you in a world of knowns than a world of unknowns. When choosing what, how and when to tell them, consider the following three things.

The right time and method to communicate

Use internal systems, processes and procedures designed to share and update information. For example, if you should be putting figures on a shared document, don't send them to your manager in an email – give them the link. If you need to communicate a delay in meeting deadlines, do it as early as possible. Telling your manager on the day that something is late, when they've been expecting it all week, does nothing for your image.

Where you can, get a step ahead on reporting back on results. When your manager is thanking you for information rather than chasing you for it, it not only puts you in a good light, it puts you in a position of power. If they have to hound you for information, they get to lay down the parameters and timelines. Taking initiative can give you control, freedom and credibility.

Choose face-to-face communication, video call, telephone call or email as appropriate. How often does an email conversation end up taking up the whole afternoon of back and forth when a five-minute call would have been much more effective and time efficient? Equally, do email if another method of communication would be an interruption or if the message needs to be recorded for future reference. If you need to make a request or discuss something at length or in detail, request the appointment with your manager but don't forget to provide a one-line indication of the purpose of the meeting. Use defined house style and branding for written communication, and set up the required backdrop for video meetings and conferencing.

Your and your manager's communication styles

Think about what makes your manager tick and what will help them to hear you. Are you telling the 'story' of the project when they want the data and stats? Are you focusing on small details when they want the big picture? They might like a direct and to-the-point approach or, conversely, be all about setting the scene and tone for a conversation.

> **Case study – the right communication style**
>
> Robin's manager could not deal with long emails. Anytime Robin sent more than a few sentences, their manager would simply ignore it (and they knew this wasn't out of laziness or spite). Ironically, Robin thought they were saving everyone meeting time by jotting down all the points in an email.
>
> Once Robin figured out what was wrong, they learned to tailor their emails for their manager. Paragraphs became bullet points; long-winded sentences became short phrases. They even challenged themselves to see how few words they could use each time. The response rate from Robin's manager rocketed!

However, don't forget your own preferences. Is there potential for a clash here? You can adjust how you communicate with others without changing who you are. Framing things in a way that appeals to your manager's communication and information preferences makes it easier for them to engage with you.

Solutions, not just problems

If you need to communicate a problem, come prepared to offer help. When you approach your manager with just the problem, that is all you are bringing to the table. The problem may not even be of your own making, but now you own it – talk about shooting yourself in the foot!

> **Top tip**
> Get caught doing the right thing. That is, make sure your manager knows when you have gone the extra mile, solved a problem without bothering them or noticed something on the horizon.

Show *evidence* of the problem. Saying 'I feel that/I believe...' isn't always enough. Your manager can't go on hearsay and speculation. Highlight the impact of the problem – on the people you serve or your organisation's activities. Bring options to resolve things, suggestions to defer to others or some questions you both may need to explore. Avoid blaming colleagues or other teams – focus on the future and the solutions.

Be careful not to become someone who bothers their manager for everything. You gain credibility when you use your initiative where you can and liaise on things only where necessary.

Case study – communicating effectively

Milo is Donor Liaison Officer at a regional charity. Due to a technical problem in the fundraising department's database, there is a delay in sending out thank-you emails to donors to the charity's latest appeal. The deadline to have contacted everyone is this coming Friday. It's currently Wednesday. Milo knows there are more and more unsent emails piling up and that donors will soon start to feel ignored and unappreciated. They head to their manager to explain things. Consider two possible approaches Milo could take:

Approach 1
Milo to their manager on Thursday afternoon: 'All the thank-you emails are in a backlog and piling up, and the team are getting really stressed because they'll miss your deadline. It's not even our fault. The database crashed – again! What shall we do?'

Approach 2
Milo to their manager on Wednesday midday: 'The database crashed around 2–4pm yesterday afternoon, which caused a backlog of thank-you emails to donors. We have worked since this morning to catch up on what we can. However, we are still exactly 70 emails behind this week's target. If we don't communicate something to them soon, they're sure to feel ignored and may withdraw future support. We don't have the capacity in the team to send out individual thank-you emails by this Friday's deadline, but we do have assurance from our IT provider that normal service is now resumed. We are going to send a group email to all donors today, with a broad thank you and explaining we will have contacted them individually by next Wednesday. That seems to be the best solution for our donors at this point. What do you think?'

You can see how the second approach communicates all the necessary information and a possible solution in a timely manner. It shows leadership, initiative and insight.

Show initiative

Keeping your manager informed on what has gone on and what is going on stands you in good stead for recognition from them. If you have your finger on the pulse, it will give you extra credibility and gravitas.

Here are a few ways you can do this:

- Read sector, industry and role-relevant journals and news. Be informed about what is going on in the wider world, and how your organisation can fit in, lead or initiate new opportunities.
- Attend sector and role-relevant events (yes, even the awkward ones) to develop relationships with possible collaborators and stay up to date on what competitors are doing.
- Choose a mentor in your sphere to work with on your career and personal development. They will have a wealth of knowledge and experience to share with you. This might be a colleague in another department – it doesn't have to be the industry guru.
- In one-to-ones, team meetings, appraisals, planning meetings and so on, share the information and knowledge you are gaining, as appropriate to the situation and conversation.
- Don't ignore what is going on *inside* your organisation. Highlight your team's, other colleagues' and other departments' projects and achievements.

> **Where next?**
> Set up a LinkedIn profile and make connections with people in your sphere and field of expertise.
>
> *www.linkedin.com*

It does not matter where in your organisation's hierarchy you are. Whether you are the most senior or most junior member of staff, there is usually opportunity to learn and share that learning somewhere in the organisation.

Chapter 3

What you need

This chapter looks at what you need from your manager in terms of your performance, authority and behavioural guidelines.

For you to be effective in your role and collaborative in your relationship with your manager, you need to be clear on some things. It's a harsh truth, but the starting point for most employee–employer relationships is that the arrangement is transactional. You will do this job, and they will give you money for doing it. You might find it hard to accept that this is the nature of working relationships, but ignoring it just puts you in a vulnerable position. You have a right to have clear communication on what you are meant to achieve and how well you are doing. Should any employee–employer dispute escalate to tribunal level and you haven't exercised this right, you will be at a disadvantage. On a more day-to-day level, if you're in a work situation where parameters, measures or rules are unclear, you will find it hard to feel confident in your role. Clarity and feedback are essential for you to perform well in your role.

The key questions you might need clarity and feedback on are:

- What results are you being measured on? What does good performance look like?

- What helps or hinders your performance that your manager can help with?
- What decision-making authority do you have?
- What behaviour and conduct are expected of you?

Your performance

Establishing measurement criteria

'What results am I being measured on?' This is not just something to ask yourself but a perfectly framed question to ask your manager. For example, as a trainer and facilitator at the Directory of Social Change, I am measured on the relationships I build, the contracts I raise and the training days I deliver. I could be perfecting slides and polishing up notes 24/7 and could surely make them more beautiful. However, the only performance measures around my slides are that they fit with house style requirements and the learning objectives of the course. I ensure that is achieved and avoid the urge to beautify slides (or save it as a treat – sad, I know).

Appraisals and one-to-one meetings are good opportunities to ask for clarity on how your results are measured. If you find these sorts of conversation challenging, there is a useful exercise for bringing up difficult questions on page 27.

Achieving results

As chapter 2 established, one of the things your manager asks of you is to fulfil your role requirements. However, there may be circumstances that create barriers to you achieving the required results. To overcome barriers, you need to be clear on the following questions:

- What is already in place to support you achieving results? Have you let your manager know this support is valued? For example, this might be short weekly meetings to agree priorities that help you to focus and organise your work.

- What is in the way of you achieving results? Have you let your manager know what barriers exist? For example, is your IT system causing problems or delays?

If your manager does not raise these points in regular communication with you, it is up to you to bring them up. I appreciate it can be daunting to approach your manager with these questions, but the reality is that the conversation needs to happen.

In chapter 1, I talked about personal power – that is, the capability to impact others through your skills, attitude and approach. Asking for what you need exerts influence, demonstrates a commitment to improvement and indicates a sense of taking responsibility. These are leadership skills and go towards improving your position power in the long term, for example by getting you recognised for promotion.

> **Top tip**
> If you are struggling with the idea of asking for help and looking stupid, weigh it up against the idea of not asking, getting things wrong and *then* looking stupid.

You can also ask for what you need on the back of providing feedback. My experience working with new and veteran managers is that feedback up the line is rarely asked for – but often needed. Giving feedback to your manager can make them see more clearly how their actions impact you. Whenever you get an opportunity to give your manager feedback, let them know what is working for you and what helps you. If they did something that helped you achieve your targets this month, if a meeting they arranged with another team meant you could do your job better, if the feedback they gave on your draft report gave you the confidence or clarity to get it finished – let them know. When you let something go unacknowledged, you

> **Top tip**
> Remind yourself that asking for the support you need to achieve results is a strength and a responsible approach to your job. Don't see it as a weakness.

risk your manager never offering that same support again (or not offering it to *you*).

I once had a manager who was really good at telling me *what* was needed. I'd get the 'what', and then go off and realise I wasn't sure where to begin. The 'what' might have been something like 'focus on meeting your income targets', but I wasn't guided as to whether, say, cold calls, network events or bulk discounts might be the best way to achieve them. We had a number of conversations around my not meeting deadlines, not delivering on targets and so on. However, things changed when I said, 'I appreciate your clarity on what is needed. You always have a clear goal and can explain the vision to me really well. But sometimes I need help with the *how* as well – first steps or a skeleton plan would help.' Abracadabra! Planning conversations were more productive, and I could use my time more efficiently – getting on with it rather than procrastinating. It was also a way for my manager to hold me to account on my delivery. My promise was: if I get the 'how', I can deliver. I felt much more in control of being able to fulfil my promise having received clear guidance to help me achieve results.

Decision-making authority

What decisions can you make and still expect the full backing of your manager? If this is unclear, you are bound to take a wrong step at some point. Clarify with your manager where the lines of decision-making authority lie: what is allowable, what is negotiable and what are the limits of your authority? I had a manager who used to say about some things, 'Always ask me first – that way I can take accountability for the outcome.' About other things, they would say, 'Act first, ask me later – I will *still* take accountability for the outcome.' It didn't matter that there were different levels of authority, just that I knew where those levels applied. Ensure conversations with your manager about decision-making cover accountability. It's all very well being given free reign, being told to 'fly, be free', but if you fly away or in the wrong direction, that leaves your manager with a problem. Therefore, having mutual clarity on decision-making and accountability is in their interests too.

> **Case study – the importance of clarity**
>
> As a fundraiser at a national charity, Kifa is responsible for income generation. This is the key area they are most closely measured on. While prioritising donor management, making applications and thanking funders, Kifa does not always get around to completing records on figures. (Notably, these records are not business-critical information but rather to monitor performance.)
>
> Kifa knows that leaving records incomplete isn't ideal, but they have limited admin time, so they focus on their key areas of work – income generation and developing new donor relationships. While Kifa's manager would like all records to be up to date all the time, the two of them agreed what Kifa should prioritise if they only have time to either update a record or make a call to a donor. Kifa gets regular reminders from their manager to update performance figures but is not 'reprimanded' for incomplete records if they can explain that more important priorities – such as thanking donors – took up their time. Both the manager and Kifa know that thanking donors is more important than completing a spreadsheet. They've agreed that Kifa can make an autonomous decision on what to prioritise if tasks are competing for limited time.

Behaviour and conduct

What do your organisation's values, code of conduct, performance standards and competencies tell you about how you should behave in your organisation and in your role?

There is an old adage that goes 'Hire for skills, fire for attitude.' This means you can hire someone who is technically competent to do the job, but you can equally train someone inexperienced to gain those same skills. It is much harder to teach someone the attitudes and conduct that will fit with your organisation's values.

Unfortunately, a poor relationship with your line manager can very easily be perceived as *your* 'poor attitude'. This is because your manager has more position power (see page 8) than you, and their voice might be louder among other people with influence in the organisation. It is not enough to just know your job and deliver on the required results – you should also know what values you are expected to uphold and what behaviours you are expected to exhibit within the organisation. In other words, *everyone* should see you doing the right thing.

Ideally, your organisation will have a code of conduct or staff handbook which outlines the behaviour expected from employees. There should be something in your job description or contract. Your HR person or department should be able to help you with this detail if you're unsure. At the very least, you can use your observation. What positive behaviours do you see in your workplace that get rewarded? This will suggest how you are expected to behave to get positive recognition.

Just as you need to be clear what you are measured on in your role competencies, you should know exactly what is expected of you in terms of behavioural conduct. While behavioural standards may differ depending on your workplace, the exercise below lists some key standards that are likely to apply in most jobs.

Behavioural standards

Score each statement on a scale of 1 (completely disagree) to 10 (completely agree).

The expected code of conduct at my workplace is clear to me.
    1 2 3 4 5 6 7 8 9 10
The measures of my conduct are clear to me.
    1 2 3 4 5 6 7 8 9 10
I meet deadlines I have agreed to.
    1 2 3 4 5 6 7 8 9 10
I deliver work to the standards outlined in my job description.
    1 2 3 4 5 6 7 8 9 10
I report on my performance clearly and in line with expectations.
    1 2 3 4 5 6 7 8 9 10
I offer solutions when raising problems.
    1 2 3 4 5 6 7 8 9 10
I am assertive and make requests or say no appropriately and professionally.
    1 2 3 4 5 6 7 8 9 10
I focus on possibilities, not limits.
    1 2 3 4 5 6 7 8 9 10
I frame problems and work on solutions in the best interests of the organisation.
    1 2 3 4 5 6 7 8 9 10
I actively seek feedback and/or other support.
    1 2 3 4 5 6 7 8 9 10
I offer feedback in a purposeful and professional way.
    1 2 3 4 5 6 7 8 9 10

The higher you score in all of these areas, the easier it will be to manage your manager. Where you score lower, consider actions you could take to improve things. For example, ensure you always meet deadlines, prepare some ideas to resolve an issue you're taking to your manager and report problems (with possible solutions) before they become crises.

Chapter 4

Structured conversations

This chapter provides approaches, frameworks and models to make difficult conversations constructive and professional.

Think about these two words: react and respond. What do you see as the distinction between them? Generally, when we react, we are 'off the cuff', driven by emotion and ill-equipped. Meanwhile, when we respond, we are considered, in emotional control, informed and prepared.

In a tricky situation, it is always helpful to buy a little time to prepare a response and avoid a reaction. The more you practice switching from reaction to response, the more natural it will become and the better the results will be.

Whenever you're faced with a difficult conversation and know you have time to prepare beforehand, plan out a suitable response – your goal, your words, the timing of your response, your questions and so on. Do this often and, eventually, even where you are put on the spot, you will be able to move to 'respond' thinking with more agility.

Conversation frameworks

Using some kind of framework can help you to have goal-focused conversations. It can also diffuse emotions – your own and others' – and convey a considered, informed approach to a difficult conversation. Try one of the tools explained below to help structure how you approach your manager.

Three-step model

Use this framework to prepare for giving someone feedback and for making requests. The three steps are:

1. Focus on the facts.
2. Focus on the fallout.
3. Focus on the future.

For example, you could apply the model to a conversation with your manager about measurable targets:

1. Fact: I haven't been given specific targets in relation to my results on relationship development.
2. Fallout: This means that I can't be sure how much time and resource to put into relationship development versus dealing with enquiries.
3. Future: Can we agree what my monthly/annual targets might look like so that I can measure this and feel I am achieving what is needed?

Plus/Delta

The Plus/Delta assessment and feedback tool is a quick and effective way to identify what works well (plus – i.e. it adds value) and what could be improved (delta – commonly used in maths to explain a change in something).

For example, if your manager tends to micro-manage, your feedback to them could go something like this: 'It's really helpful that you are to hand and supportive with my work. [plus] What would help me sometimes is to work independently and report back on key areas you'd like to monitor. [delta] I think that would free up a bit more time for both of us. And you could let me know what, when and how to report back. Do you agree?'

Effective questions

It is sometimes said that you can't change someone's mind without asking them a question. However, ask the wrong question and you might get the wrong answer. When faced with a difficult conversation, it can be hard to frame a question without it sounding loaded, hostile or cynical. If you need to challenge or question your manager, make sure you get the question right. A few things make a question effective:

- using non-judgmental and non-leading language and tone;
- being direct without apologising for your question;
- asking at the right time and in the right place.

For example, take this question asked right at the end of a meeting: 'So, sorry if this is a stupid question, but now we've talked about it all, are we just to go ahead and implement it without even talking to the marketing team?'

The question clearly has an agenda and carries a certain tone of judgement. Imagine, instead, the following question being asked at the start of the meeting: 'Can we agree at the end of our discussion how we will keep the marketing team informed of any decisions and action points, please?'

There's an old saying that goes 'Judge a person not by the answers they give but by the questions they ask.' For collaborative and positive relationships, effective questioning is a useful skill to develop. Not only does it usually help progress things more quickly, but it helps manage emotions and knee-jerk reactions. For one, an effective question usually means you have given it some consideration (which means you slowed down, analysed, reflected and planned). Although sometimes you might have to pose a question quickly – on the spot at a meeting, say – usually you can plan what is called a 'clean' question (i.e. one that is free of judgement, is not leading or loaded, and progresses the conversation). The following exercise helps you to take your original question and reframe it to make it clean and ensure it lands well with others.

> **Top tip**
> You may want to make a statement that could feel insensitive or awkward. Can you reframe it as a question? A genuine question – not a facetious one!

Reflection exercise

Consider tricky situations you have to deal with that involve your manager: being asked to do more work, being micro-managed, not getting support, being overlooked for opportunities and so on. Think about what questions you'd like to ask them and use the process described below to plan some effective questions to get a productive discussion going around the issue. Write down a question you would like to ask your manager. You can start as blunt as you like, such as 'Why the hell are you like this?' Work through the following reflections to help you clean up your question:

- **Consider how your question might land.** Will it cause offence, defensiveness, confusion or even withdrawal from discussion? Does it provide the person with the opportunity to give you the information you need? Does the question trap them into an answer or back them into a corner?
- **What is your purpose in asking this question?** What outcome are you expecting? Do you want them to take action? Do you want to get an idea taken on board?
- **How likely is it that the question will help you achieve your desired outcome?** Will it cause further confusion, conflict or problems?
- **How might you rephrase the question?** Try re-writing your question, ensuring you keep it focused on the future, solutions and goals.

- **Check the question for 'trigger' words (e.g. 'with respect' or 'obviously'), judgement and ambiguity.** Repeat the steps above until you're satisfied you've come up with a clean question.

Going through this process might change 'Why the hell are you like this?' to 'Can I ask what has caused your response to this situation?' or something similar that can open the possibility to having a productive discussion.

Tips for asking effective questions

- Use **single questions**. It's very tempting to string multiple questions together to get someone to see the whole problem. In fact, it usually just confuses them, misleads them or causes them to only answer the first or last question. Keep things simple with a single question to start.

- Use **probing questions**. They will help you to gain understanding. Say things like 'You mentioned X – can you tell me more about that?' or 'What are your thoughts/feelings/views on Y so far?'

- Use **link questions**. These are useful to move people on from a certain point to another. They include things like 'That's useful/interesting. In relation to that, can I ask...?'

- Use **comparison questions**. If you are getting conflicting messages from your manager, such questions can be helpful. For example, 'As I understood it, last time we met you said X. Now the situation is Y. Could you please explain the difference so I am clear with what is needed now?'

- Use **one-thing questions**. Such questions lead to securing commitment or getting specific details. For instance, 'What is one thing you would like me to do more of/differently?' or 'What one thing could I do to be considered for promotion next time?'

- Use **open questions**. These are useful if you need to find out more – 'Can you tell me more about the promotion criteria?'

- Use **closed questions**. These are helpful to find out specifics – 'Are there specific criteria for promotion to senior researcher?'

Chapter 5

Building resilience

This chapter looks at where and how you can source support when things get difficult.

Nobody should have to go to work expecting to come home feeling belittled, undervalued or undermined. Our work is often such a large part of our life, and it is important that we have some sense of power and control there. Trying some of the approaches and strategies outlined so far will give you more leverage in your line-management relationship and allow you to feel some control over the outcome. However, they are not a fix-all solution. These are things you can *try* in order to receive different results and responses from your manager. Unfortunately, in some situations, nothing you try has an influence on someone else. What's the solution then? There are tactics and resources to help you manage when it all becomes too much.

Bullying and harassment

Under no circumstances is it OK for someone to be bullied or harassed at work. If you believe you are being bullied or harassed by your manager, it can seem like your options are limited – you might not be able to simply speak to your manager after all!

Examples of bullying or harassment at work might include the following:
- someone spreading rumours or lies about you;
- always being hushed and put down in meetings;

- having your work constantly criticised;
- having an unfair workload in relation to your counterparts;
- being excluded from social events.

While there is no legal definition for bullying, there is one for harassment. Bullying becomes harassment when it relates to one or more of the relevant protected characteristics under the Equality Act 2010. The protected characteristics are: age, disability, gender reassignment, marriage and civil partnership, pregnancy and maternity, race, religion or belief, sex and sexual orientation.

If you think you are being bullied or harassed at work, please do not sit in silence. There are three practical things you can do:

1. Seek to address the problem informally first. This might mean a chat with your manager if that seems possible for you or with a colleague who can support you to take the next steps.
2. If you don't get a resolution through an informal approach, follow your organisation's grievance procedure to raise your concern. Consult your staff handbook (or similar document) for guidance on standards, protocols and policies around this.
3. Contact your HR department and/or trade union representative.

Managing stress

Some stress is OK – in fact, it can be positive. 'Good' pressure gets us out of bed in the morning, motivates us to have a productive day and helps us dig deep when we are tired or flaking. However, long-term pressures without light at the end of the tunnel can lead to burnout and poor mental health. Using the following stress-management approaches can help you to avoid such outcomes:

- **Develop awareness.** Identify things that are likely to trigger your stress. It might be emails piling in or noise in the background when you are working. Whatever yours are, you might not be able to avoid the situation itself, but you can prepare to manage your feelings and well-being when your stress is triggered. Learn to notice your stress symptoms – we all have different early signs. Do you become short tempered or prone to crying more? Are you over-eating/smoking/indulging or neglecting yourself? Be aware of those signs so that you can nip things in the bud before stress builds to excessive pressure.

- **Take action.** Remove your stress triggers where you can, and where you can't, identify ways to manage your feelings. Do you have regular email clean-ups? Can you wear headphones at your desk? Practice stress management techniques such as mindful breathing, yoga and similar low-impact exercises. Focus on identifying the first step you can take rather than trying to solve the whole problem at once.

- **Use active distraction.** This doesn't mean burying your head in the sand but finding things that take your mind off whatever is stressing you. It's about not taking stress home with you when you leave the office or desk. There is little comfort in sitting on the sofa all evening, stressing about what your manager has said or done to you today. To gain relief and perspective, do something distracting and purposeful – take a long walk listening to music, start that creative project you always wanted to or reorganise some storage.

> **Where next?**
>
> CALM helpline (5pm to 12am, every day): 0800 585858 (telephone) or visit thecalmzone.net.
>
> If stress is impairing your ability to function or sleep, or you are having intensely worrying thoughts, don't delay seeking professional medical help.

Resilience

Resilience is the ability to function well in the face of adversity. It stands you in good stead to deal with problems and challenges which recur when trying to manage your manager. I consider the following to be key characteristics of resilience. Take some time to reflect on how you could incorporate them into your work life and actions.

- **Taking a positive view.** You don't have to pretend things are good when they aren't. Taking a positive view means seeing possibilities rather than limits. Rather than telling yourself, 'I can't do anything about this', ask yourself, 'What can be done?' Rather than apportioning blame and focusing on the past, seek solutions and focus on the future.
- **Taking action.** It is said that the best thing to do is the right thing, the second-best thing to do is the wrong thing and the worst thing to do is nothing at all. By doing something, you change a situation and progress things. Take action by identifying small starting steps, defining longer-term goals of where you want things to be and deciding what measures you can put in place to manage your stress and well-being.
- **Engagement.** In resilience terms, being engaged is about dedication, commitment and enthusiasm. Set your own goals, expectations and boundaries, and commit to them. Engagement sets us up to navigate and overcome challenges more effectively.
- **Adaptability.** This refers to being versatile in your mindset to accept the things you cannot change and having flexibility in your actions to change the things you can. Adaptability means you can adjust to changing environments and situations, cope with a change of plan and adjust your communication approach to suit someone else's needs.

Final note

The most important point highlighted in this book is that it's all about managing the relationship, not about changing who you or your manager are. Keep this in mind when you hit bumps or things don't work out on the first try – it can take a few attempts to get things right and see the impact. In the short term, things can feel awkward or frustrating, but the long-term rewards of managing your manager are a happier you, a trusting manager and a more successful performance for you both.